best new poets

2005

G<small>EORGE</small> G<small>ARRETT</small>, E<small>DITOR</small>

Jeb Livingood, Series Editor

This book was published by Samovar Press, Charlottesville, Virginia,
in cooperation with *Meridian,* www.readmeridian.org. For additional information
on *Best New Poets,* see our Web site at www.bestnewpoets.org.

Cover photograph of Devon Sproule, www.devonsproule.com
by Aaron Farrington, www.aaronfarrington.com

Text set in Adobe Garamond Professional

Manufactured in the United States of America

Library of Congress Control Number: 2005901554

ISBN 0-9766296-0-7
ISSN 1554-7019

Contents

Introduction

Welcome to *Best New Poets*, an annual anthology of fifty poems from emerging writers. In these pages, the term "emerging writer" has a narrow definition: here, it means someone who has yet to publish a book-length collection of poetry. Like the rules for many anthologies, that one is, perhaps, arbitrary. But the main goal of *Best New Poets* is to provide special encouragement and recognition to new poets, the many writing programs they attend, and the magazines that publish their work.

From April to June of 2005, *Best New Poets* accepted nominations from each of these sources. For a small reading fee, writers could upload two poems to a Web site, www.bestnewpoets.org, as part of our Open Competition. A month earlier, writing programs from around the United States and Canada had sent nominations of up to two writers, whom *Best New Poets* later solicited for work. And the anthology also asked literary magazines across North America to send two of their best recent poems by writers who met our definition of "emerging." We asked that the poems submitted either be unpublished or published after June 15, 2004. So, not only do new writers appear in this anthology, you're seeing some of their most recent work.

In all, we received submissions from nearly 600 poets, with some 1,100 poems uploaded to our system. A pool of readers blindly ranked the submissions, and seventy finalists went on to this year's editor, George Garrett, for his final winnowing to fifty. In this first installment of *Best New Poets,* we were especially pleased that almost half of our final selections came from the Open Competition. Two of those Open Competition poets, Randall Couch and Lauren Rusk, also received cash prizes for their outstanding work.

As with any anthology, this was a team effort.

My special thanks go to George Garrett. His generosity to emerging writers is legendary, and his enthusiasm for poetry, boundless. He served as editor of this year's anthology for free, donating his time and advice, and *Best New Poets 2005* would not have been possible without him.

The same goes for the reading pool—Kevin McFadden, Angie Hogan, Alexis Luckey, and Ryan Fox—all of them amazing poets.

Special thanks to Lisa Russ Spaar, Director of the University of Virginia's Graduate Creative Writing Program, whose encouragement helped make this anthology a reality. I also want to acknowledge the many support staff in Bryan Hall, specifically June Webb, Lois Payne, Cheryll Lewis, and Guinn Baker, whose efforts kept *Best New Poets 2005* humming along—and the bills paid.

The University of Virginia Librarian, Karin Wittenborg, also played a significant role, both in her support of *Meridian* and for this project, as did English Chair Gordon Braden, whose signature went on many a grant application.

At a time when some argue the influence of poetry is in decline, there are, in fact, more books of poetry published today than ever before. While many large publishing houses and media outlets no longer feature poetry, a growing number of small presses and magazines still believe in its power—and its necessity.

Count us among them. We're proud to bring you fifty poets whose work makes that belief easy to come by.

—*Jeb Livingood*

Ellen Wehle

Reincarnation

Buddha said, Be a lamp unto yourself.

In every storefront I pass, the telltale flicker.
Smudged pentimento of my face . . . some study from another

day, when the master raised his brush to more ambition.
Meanwhile the industry of sunlight grinds out June.

Blackflies as cantata, the thousand seed pods whirling.
Observed all afternoon by the great clock

that hovers like an eye above town, I need to know
I happened. This went down.

—Open Competition Winner

Sally Molini

Silk Shop on the Ganges

Varanasi

Chant drifts in through the window
and I can see the swaddled bodies,
empty of what held them here.
Even at this distance I'd rather not watch
the blunt alchemy,
bone dissolved to flame,
earth uncurled, its tenuous states
of odor, ash and smoke
vanishing above the river
as Ranjit brings the scarves,
holds them up one by one,
each square half air,
half liquid prism.
Color cool to the touch,
just enough fabric
for a wisp of dye.
I buy six. As he wraps them,
he tells how, after the *Bombyx mora*
spins its cocoon, the silk farmer

kills the chrysalis with a shot of steam
so its struggle to emerge
won't damage the precious thread.
He smiles, hands me the package,
promising the scarves will never bleed.

—Open Competition Winner

Gary Joseph Cohen

Lepidopteraphile

It used to be that the music of drainpipes
Choking down rainwater was enough
To keep me liquored up and mean-mouthed,
      my hands hooked

In lilacs long enough to dry my scales of dew,
And the mornings hot enough to pull my good leg
Up through laundry lines and elm bramble
      one slim foot at a time.

If I had been raised any other way
I would have taken longer to shimmy
Between the boulders in the backyard for warmth
      and comfort—

I couldn't be the moth I am: wide-eyed and tight-lipped,
Sleeping until noon with my legs crossed,
Tapping on your window at night
      with the gray feathers of my bald head—

I wouldn't be lighting on your black hair as I do now,
Nestling in the wooden porch of your ear, waiting
    for your bulb to flicker on for the evening.

—*Open Competition Winner*

Chip Livingston

Burn

That owl was an omen
Driving home from the airport
Not once but twice
It rose in my headlights
From rain black asphalt
Great white wings nearly touching
Windshield wipers   that low flying escort
Stretching sixty miles toward Alabama
The owl was always right
Something died and something else
Was just about to
I checked my daughter's red-eye slumber
In the rearview mirror
No need to worry her with divination
An hour drive delayed by rain
And now this trepidation on the slick black road
Certain as miscarried fortune
Her coming home to Mama in an autumn storm
And no such thing as California
Just a red clay creekbed down the road
From the house I birthed her in

Filling up to bathe away a sorrow
Blinking lights behind us
Before I hear the sirens
Firetruck passes on the narrow bridge
Then Crabtree Church in flames beyond the graveyard
My daughter wakes and guesses lightning
But I never heard the thunder crack
And only saw the lightning white of dreaded wings
I pull in   step out   and open an umbrella
Stand with the firemen   watch the frame fall down
The Marshal asks if we saw anything
Like kids driving away in a four-wheeler
They found tracks in the mud
Whiskey and beer bottles   a gas can
Burn! All those years of homecoming
Annual dinners on the grounds
Hymns around a weather-warped piano
Burn! My granddad's Indian education
Walls that heard a thousand lessons
A thousand prayers in high soprano
Burn! Fifty paper funeral parlor fans
Cokesbury hymnals and sixteen pews
Reduced to flakey carbon tamped with rain
The death of wood and glass
And half a baby's ashes in my daughter's pocketbook
All the little names we'll never sing
I aim to find that messenger again and scare him off
Litter the road with his insolent feathers

—Nominated by Ploughshares

Temple Cone

One Crow, a Killing

The men who kill crows know their acts bear
no repeal. Waiting till dusk, they grip
twelve-gauges loaded with shot
and watch the sky for murders
circling the cornfields. A single crow
can ride a stalk to ground,
pry open the husk, the veined silk,
scraped kernels peppering its face
with flecks of white and gold.

The farmers I know won't let them near
the corn, but shoot before they perch.
Some, though, will walk in behind
to see those damned eyes, the iris red
beneath a sheen of black
and kill them when they try to rise.
With wings stretched out like funeral crepe
they nail them to a fence.

I've seen it done. I've brought crows out
from the cornrows, the weight of each in hand

swinging with my stride as I walk.
"Nothing but a warning," farmers say, "to keep
them out the corn." No matter how the eye
squints, the bodies of crows mark fences
like blood scrawled on a door.
In a week they dry, black down puffing out
and caught in the wind like milkweed,
blackness iridescent as scales,
the skin too weak to hold.

                                   I've seen
what else is done to them in death.
Feet cut off, poked through
and threaded with string for wind chimes,
the talons clicking hollowly
as crystal. And at Sunday service
when choir and preacher begin to sing,
motes of dust falling like gold in heat,
the women fan themselves with coal-dark wings.

—Open Competition Winner

Lauren Rusk

Adrift at Notre Dame

1.

The organ resounds within   this hollow mountain,
chaos rolls forth,

           the hand of creation
works upon the darkness,

             rumbling my chest,
the instrument's   instrument.

Here so soon after

          enfolding silence,
familiar though Parisian,

          the Quaker meeting
where I dozed, then   flailed awake

to noon to stumble

         into all this...

            folderol,
I would have said.

2.

French burbles from the pulpit,

                                easy to ignore

when you get only scraps,

                        except *"Le Seigneur"*...

But I didn't come to cavil

                      at *les masculins et féminins,*

rather, to feel

                what I can.

3.

The priest looks kindly

                  in my direction

as though at a grandchild.

                      I hear

"vous imaginez"...

                "mystère"...

"aimer," to love;

            why not

give up this problem of belief?

                    Just feel—

but through the senses   there's the rub.

For me, the spirit stirs

in the trees,
in a painting,
in a face—

an old Quaker woman's
furrowed peace.

Maybe even here—
the glass-struck light,
these greens and blues,

gold and scarlet fashioned into . . .

Now he's angry.
The finger jabs:
impératifs du papa.

But then, *"Enfin,"*
the congregants turn
and give one another
"la paix,"
the handshake,
touch
what is, what is not.

4.

Around the vast perimeter,
altars, alcoves—one unlit,
a jumble of storage
we're supposed to glide by.

A single stone tenant
reclines on a dais
as they seem often to do.
Some understanding has come to him.

He lifts a gentle hand to tell it
        to the chairs,
    the scaffolding and coils of wire,
the foolish bubble wrap
                foaming from its box,
the vacuum machine . . .

5.

A donkey pokes his nose out
from a frieze called *Le mystère
de l'humanité du Christ.*
Providing the flight from Egypt,
he gazes at me abstractedly,
ears pricked as if he hears—
what? and wonders why he's there.
Among many gospel figures

the donkey stands out—his head
the highest relief.
I love
his obscurity,
the way he loiters
in the now,
his sensitive muzzle
inviting—though it's not permitted—
touch.

—Open Competition Prize Winner

John Hennessy

Why Not Dig Up the Dog?

> *I see by your eagerness…that you expect to be informed*
> *of the secret with which I am acquainted; that cannot be.*
> —Mary Shelley, *Frankenstein*

Why not dig up the dog? What parent's not
Part hypocrite? To wit, he's bone and leather,
A Giacometti we can't make animate
With plug and socket, son. He's dead forever.

I'd be a monster not to sweeten it some:
Let old bones fertilize; our setter flies
With angels—that's not him, that stick of dumb
Brown calcium. Of course I sympathize,

Although by now our dog's more dogwood bloom,
A calla lily. The rest is heresy,
And hard to undo—that *soul's* an empty room
Or shorthand for a jolt of electricity.

—*Open Competition Winner*

Cody Walker

Bozo Sapphics

Bozo, Toe to Toe

Tilt the glass: the terrorist turns to freedom
Fighter. Likewise, clowns, in the funhouse mirror,
Stand as kings. Self-interested theories on which
Bozo calls bullshit.

Bozo's Imbroglio

Showmen, offered tenderness, tend to take it.
Husbands know this. Tickle a clown: does he not
Laugh? Then why subpoena him, why inflict more
Pricks on this Bozo?

Bozo, Woe

Bozo's six apologies, five excuses,
Four rebuffs, and three switcheroos are met by
Two deaf ears. Behaviorists gather, call this
First-order clowning.

Rebozos

Scarves, of ample length, that are brightly dyed and
Chiefly worn by Mexican women. Not a
Further Bozo. Not an attempt at cloning.
Shudder to think it.

Bozo, Quid Pro Quo

Names, he knows. Our Bozo can cough up names till
Cows croak. Ask for names in return, however . . .
Same-old same-old: "Bundle" (in Old High German),
"Big Mouth" (in Latin).

Bozo Utters a Bon Mot

Asked about increasingly vitriolic
Spats regarding Comedy's tragic center,
Bozo cries, "Ridiculous quibberdicking!
HA ha ha." [Weeping.]

Bozo, Incognito

He's the older guy in the hat. Or wait—the
Tap instructor (cane and corsage) about to
Pay his tab. Or Bartender Joe. Good Jesus!
Everywhere: Bozo.

—Open Competition Winner

Kevin A. González

Cultural Slut

You narrow it down to three—
the first episode of *South Park,*
the first time you read Sharon Olds,
& the Field Day spent under the bleachers
with Victoria, your fingernails
becoming taxis of her scent, her pupils
disappearing like marbles into a grate.
At nine, you asked your father
about the rusted dispenser
screwed into the men's room at Duffy's
& Scotch sprayed through his nose.
You fingered the change slot
& fed it your pinball allowance
but nothing came out.
It was Sharon Olds who killed you
with *the father's cock & the mother's cunt,*
the cartoon probes & pelvis-spills
what shocked you, Victoria's tang
on your nails after tug of war,
the one you skipped & told your teammates
your fingers were crossed *for them.*

These are the boulevards you cannot rip
from your eyes. There was the Lucky Seven
& Naranjito, *La Chica Fuego,*
a cigarette puckered between her labia,
loops of smoke twirling out
like an exorcism before a neon backdrop.
All this at fifteen, plaid skirts
cutting you off in school hallways.
Your father's invisible son, Pepito,
was a day older than you
& hit the buzzer shots you missed,
held his breath longer underwater.
Remember when you brought Victoria home
& your father said Pepito
had already fucked her? And your first time,
how she bled, & you thought
you'd murdered the prodigal son,
the condom drowned
in the eye of the toilet's undertow?
None of it matters. Not your father's
sagging gray lungs or the naive
objectification of your title.
You've narrowed it down to three—
& wouldn't we like to see Cartman
slugging it out with Sharon Olds,
& isn't Victoria a name you've made up
to protect the identity of C.,
& wasn't C. a slut
for skipping away with the ethics teacher,
the cross on her necklace

swaying like a silver pendulum,
& didn't you buy her that cross
with your pinball allowance, which was
surely a bill cheaper than Pepito's?
When you first taught creative writing
& assigned a "How To" poem,
a girl with a tongue stud wrote
"How To Fuck an English Teacher
for a Good Grade," & her first line read,
"Write a 'How To Fuck an English Teacher
for a Good Grade' poem." Maybe
your mouth watered, & maybe
you read Sharon Olds to the class
& said, *if you can't write sex like this*
you can't write sex at all, & yes, you are
older now & going against that,
narrowing it down to three
though none of it matters. Not the cherry-
flavored chapstick or C.'s number
in the phonebook, 787-4797.
Not your life, that instant between
the last seven & the first ring. Not
how you hang up & she punches star-69
& you retreat from the accusing phone.

—*Nominated by* Hotel Amerika

Valerie Bandura

Vagina and Cross-Cocks

For the flag,
      they sliced a pair of white boxers, and on it,
            in marmalade,

outlined the diamond shape of a vagina
          slightly open
      with wisps around the lips for the pubic hair,
            and under that,

a pair of erect penises
      criss-crossed
        like two femur bones under a skull,

clipped the shorts to a flagpole and hoisted the thing
          flapping
            into the eggshell blue air.

        Excuse me,
I would have begun with a narrative,
      with the houseboat rented by five older couples

who went a little slaphappy or skunk-drunk
                              or both for one week on Lake Powell
                                        to steer clear of

what everyone wanted to hear
                    not one more word about—
                                        the children

lost to what the doctors don't yet know
                to call, the summer of the cancer, the winter
                                of divorce, and how

                the hell they ever got from that country to

this one, and then were forced to learn the language
                                of middle age,
                                        then old age—

I would have started there
                had their friendship somehow clarified
                                the image waving above their heads: a silly

sign of fornication and death,
                        lust and loss,
                                two Great Absolutes

born of the same primal impulse:
                        to pronounce the self
                                against a dying life in a desperate

gesture against surrender

on a house that's really a boat

on a lake that's really a desert

where they again are untouched and intact and can

still make love

to a world decent and just,

like fireflies

dying on the ground,

but still blinking:

fuck me, fuck me.

—*Open Competition Winner*

Laurie Stoll

In the Details

Call forth for me
the small gods of unwinding,
the gods of question, of disillusion,
of dissolution, of picking apart.

Call forth the nimble gods
who spear dimness,
who trample rigid crystals,
whistle ripples down through concretions of damp.

Call forth the god
of the pluck of strong fingers,
rasping at bindings, prying at junctions,
the husker, who splits out each naked seed.

Call for me, call forth the gods
who unravel. They loose the whole cloth into contrary winds,
yards on yards billowing, rampant and sheening, a flood
on the ache of clean sand.

—Nominated by Streetlight

Leslie Shipman

Woman in the Snow, Berlin, New York, 1992

for Andrea Yates

A woman stands in the snow
in a pale flannel nightgown

in midday,
and the light is bright and angry.

She is burning her bed in the front yard.

There's a barren lilac bush bent
beneath a thin whisper of frost

and behind the garage
an old wheelbarrow
filled with broken tools.

Her hair is a rip of orange,
unwashed and neglected
like the children she left inside

in a bowl
in front of the TV

where the sleepy blue light
lullabies
an infinite expanse of daytime.

The cops wonder how
she got the bed out of the house.

"On my back,"
she tells them,

the frame, the mattress,
the chattering bedclothes
and oily blankets,

all of it fit for the fire,

the flames more beautiful
than any she's ever seen,

like the blaze of a falling angel
or Jesus reaching out
his bleeding palm for hers,

the rescue
she's been waiting for
come at last,

come when she called
out loud.

—Open Competition Winner

Beth Bachmann

Another Poem about Memphis Rocking

> *A lot of people thinks that the devil has come here.*
> —account of the New Madrid Earthquakes, 23 January 1812

Only the devil can turn water
against its course, bring a lake

to a boil by stomping time
with his reel foot. The devil's roots

reach as deep as the swamp cypress
and are not so easily overturned.

There are two things in this world
you can't put a price on:

whiskey after a storm,
a mean harmonica draw.

A soul, on the other hand,
I can get you cheap. I know plenty.

Give me the screams of animals,
the Mississippi bellowing

from the bottomlands
into the blue, blue south.

—*Nominated by* The Southern Review

Thomas Park

Countryfied

I moved south; I was young; times was hard for northern black folk, still
When my Mama was scared I might get strung out on dope, Superfly could cope, Shaft
    was in Africa, but the *Good Times* had not rolled. I moved to Carolina

When I didn't know nothing about segregation, or the Klan, I didn't know I was colored
    When "Big Ma" and Granddaddy were the world to me, man,

When I wanted to smell the mimosa trees, run in two-acre yards, and buy a Coke/12 cent.
    When I was just a fat colored kid whose folks didn't want him to see the city burn,

When I moved down south, last thing I wanted to be was country, but I was countryfied.
    When I used to catch snakes and keep 'em, and fly "doo doo" bugs on a string,

When my eyes got "dotted," and I had a knot yanked in my ass,
    When I swung over the "holla'" like Tarzan on "Muskiedine" vines

When I remembered to get the "red dirt" off my shoes, and got used to 2nd-class schooling
    When my nose got wide open, and I had a scrap yard behind my barn,

When I learned to cluck a mule, plow a tractor, and used pokeberries for blood,
    When I "primed 'bacca" for Mr. Tom, a good man, and "Red Jenkins"/Po' bastard.

When I picked cucumbers, peppers, cotton, and grapes, after the Mexicans came,
    When I cut down trees, busted wood, and killed a barnyard hen for dinner /1 time

When I chased naked young girls through the woods to my "honey hush,"
    When I ate "nigger toes" at Christmas, and brains with my grits /1 time,

When I said, "yes, sir" to some man who didn't deserve it, and hated myself,
    When every Saturday after Thanksgiving was for Blood Sport

When I could make a sam'ich with pimento cheese, banana, or tomatoes,
    When I threw apple peelings at pig pickings, and parties on the creek

When I said, "yes, ma'am" to some woman who didn't deserve it, and hated myself.
    When I worked for nothing, or little, and took it

When I didn't have a pot to piss in, or a window to throw it out,
    When I learned "wrunt" meant ruined, and "ranch" meant wrench

When I ate polk salad in my greens /1 time,
    When "rock candy" and "moonshine" was my flu cure.

When I believed the lynching tales were the truth, and thought black was a'bad
    When I called Crack " The Hard," Crystal "The Iiiice," and was afraid to wear my Kufi,

When I was high as "Coony Brown," and U were "tight as a tick"
    When down east ended at Okrakoke, and I didn't mind ol' glory flyin' in Raleigh

When I was willing to recast a mended bucket in a shallow pond,
    When my neighbors shared their fresh produce with me, and I grew some to share.

When I left to get a job with Ford and I called Warrenton home.

—Nominated by Wayne State University

Peter Kline

The Sphinx

We see it from the forest road—a church
crouched above three centuries of dead,
treeshadow huge against the granite haunch.
I take your gloved hand just beyond the flood.

Knowing ourselves mistaken, luckless, strange,
we await the fatal question. Nothing comes.
Tomorrow, the *Ave* of a winter wedding:
these doors will open for the bride and groom.

—Open Competition Winner

Randall Couch

Apostrophe to Violetta

> *Tra voi saprò dividere*
> *Il tempo mio giocondo*
>   —Piave (*La Traviata*, act I)

I couldn't help it, feeling like you—
        leaving my city friends
                for a life I'd stopped hoping for.
Yet there he was, sweet and strange
        as a country apple, sound.
After the film at the Varsity
        under Zeffirelli's marquee
                the lights of Paris dazzled me
and I forgot the Kindly Ones.

I camped a swoon, backhand to brow:
        Would you love me better
                if I were consumptive,
                a courtesan on a chaise?

Even now I want to take it back.
God, I knew better. My mother's
        pebbled breast—but that's the thing:
I'd always thought it would be cancer.

His answer *No* was perfect.
I've never found disease
       erotic. I loved him for it.
I heard: *Be easy, you are enough.*
And in the lights I hummed
       Libiamo—ah,
I could still sing then.

Don't think the diagnostic irony
      after seven years,
           another city,
      was lost on me.

So here it is: *Mycobacterium avium*
      acts on the lungs
like *Mycobacterium TB*—
      except for one or two things,
      except it's rare, except
there are no good drugs.
Medical science has no answer,
      said a dog-eyed doctor
      to the question
      Why me?

Let's get this out of the way.
We had hope, the disease was slow,
      research was enterprising.
But he never reminded me of that swoon
      and I never replayed my line
      or his reply.

Do you know how sweet
his quiet breathing sounds at night?

I write like hell.
I bake. I burrow
              into this life until
                        I can't be dislodged.
I don't live sick.
I tell myself it's therapeutic.
It is erotic.

Now that he's learned to give
              injections, he plays
              darts on my ass.
Good for my spirits, but what
              if he starts to enjoy it?
*Let's take a weekend away
              down in New Castle*, I say.
There'll be time,
              he offers, *in the fall.*

I punch the pillows when he's not home.

When I was a child we played a game.
              What would you do
                        with six months to live?

I'll cash the retirement funds
              for Paris and emeralds,
              frame my pale skin in opera gowns.

But already I can't sit silent through a single act
      and there's no glamour in shame.

Violetta,
      were you wise after all
    to give your fortune
        for a simple season
        in a small house?

O come son mutata!

I watch that open face,
      what it learns to look at
      without hardening.
I have this tube now under my arm,
      a fistula to drain the lung.
He opens my blouse
      and lifts the gauze pad,
      probes the fouled tube
      with a clean swab.
All he seems to want is more
      of what we have,
        the dwindling daily me.

Sometimes I have to turn my eyes
      from such tenderness.

—Open Competition Prize Winner

Judith Cox

Mojacar, Spain

I. 8:30 A.M.

Light slants through French doors, spills across black and white tiles from a Vermeer.
Sebastiano squats under the solitary palm tree, patiently watering. The hose dangles
from one hand, a cigarette burns in the other. Dates red as cayenne,
yellow as turmeric wither at his feet.
Lupo, the Pharaoh hound, lies panting in the sun at the studio door.
This is how the day starts.

II. Pomegranate Grove

Some fall to the ground unripe, untouched.
Some lie withered, passed over.
Others hold to the vine, split by the sun, ravaged by birds.
Still more wait, crimson from the urging of swollen seeds.

III. Impenetrable

The wall of prickly pear grows deep and wild.
Only a fool would touch an agave fence.
You take the fruit from my hand, throw it to the ground.

Very dangerous. Many tiny needles.
Your fingers glide along my palm, barely touching.
What do you feel?
Everything.

IV. Marking

"Squirrel," you say, showing me a fine-haired brush from India.
"They don't kill the animal, they catch it, take a few hairs."
You dip the tip in red ocher, stroke the back of my neck.
Just this touch and the wind in the pepper trees.

—*Open Competition Winner*

Brian Brodeur

To a Young Woman in a Hospital Bed

It starts with an urge, she says, innocent
enough: clipping her fingernails
to the cuticle, paper cuts

she slits along her hands, or slicing up
her arms in homeroom with a plastic knife
to scare the gawking boys.

Eraser burns: those competitions
to see which of her girlfriends
flinches first as she scrapes the rubber

edges across her forearms,
biting down hard on a wooden ruler
so she doesn't scream, or stop.

Then she gets good at it; she always wins.
She does it on her own, and it feels good
rubbing the eraser over the black scabs,

trying to wipe away her own skin.
She experiments then with safety pins:
pricking the soft flesh

between index finger and thumb, piercing
each side of the thin skin that
pops like bubble wrap.

She fastens them, sticking in
five at a time, all in a row, and watches them
throbbing in a kind of dance.

She calls it the Silver-Lady Dance,
showing her friends who laugh
but cringe after she forces the eighth pin

through. And this is how she knows
something about her is wrong,
carving the names

or rock bands into her thighs
with her stepfather's
box-cutter: *Poison, Aerosmith*—

it doesn't matter, it just feels better
cutting words instead of marks
that don't mean anything.

And this suffices, this becomes
what life is; burn by burn, pressing a hot
clothes-iron against her arm,

lifting it to let the steam breathe out
and pressing it down again, longer this time,
harder, as the burning fills the hall.

Minutes go by. Hours. And she feels
nothing. It's like she's burning
someone else's skin, letting the steaming metal

peel away the flesh, scorching it.
She watches the skin singe, the muscle
bubble, but she still can't feel a thing.

So she stops. She wraps the arm in gauze
and goes on with her day, even forgetting
what made her want to do that to herself.

And in a way this makes it all
worth it: the fever, the infection, the dizzy
drive to the ER she hardly remembers,

the morphine drip and intern psych-major
who asks her questions from the standard form
(even flirting with her a little),

the swell of pride she feels turning over
to show the scars—the deepest ones, the ones
branded on her back not even she has seen.

—Nominated by George Mason University

Kristin Abraham

Little Red Riding Hood Missed the Bus

Somewhere they won't know
she got herself lost.
But she's folding paper sparrows
inside her head; she's trying confession:
Things moving. The corner of my eye.

The camera is above her;
the angle looks down on her small
red twirling. But sometimes
the camera is in her eyes. We see the
everywhere she looks—
                    face—

Now she can't even see the trees
for all the forests. Somewhere a log cabin,
a woodstove. The first fantasy was a mistake.
The second had a rag stuffed in its mouth.

—Nominated by West Virginia University

Joanna Pearson

Personals

i.

You, the moon; me, the sun.
You, the steam off jasmine tea;
me, the radio from another room.
Come and listen to me.

ii.

I won't lie. I'm tired and lonely
and tired of being lonely
and tired of bearing the rough beast
of myself, its dull slump,
through the world with nothing
but bemused, witty ironies.
We can talk over dinner, awkwardly.

iii.

October on the prep school lawn
and the girls are playing soccer.

The late light skims their faces,
the ribbons on their ponytails flutter,
they pump their tawny arms
across the green yard.
See the whites of their jerseys,
the long line of their leg muscles.
I am old, too old to join them,
I wasted youth on self-consciousness.
Mature man seeking eighteen year old.

iv.

I saw you in the grocery store.
We had a conversation—
Remember? The carrots in my hand?
A box of cereal, some fruit, my crooked tooth?
I think you smiled at my poorly told joke,
but I didn't get your name.

v.

Divorced mother of two,
kind heart for strays
and brute men who
remind me of my ex-husband.
Rough voices, hard hands,
the lulling presence of their hate.

vi.

Picture me at seventeen on a beach with friends.
Late summer: slim, fine tan shoulders.
I ran like the wind and loved books, travelling,
the Motown from my brother's stereo,
and flowers dripping in the flower stands.
I swear, I was beautiful then and loved so many things.
Attractive middle-aged woman,
interests wide-ranging.

vii.

I could write you many words
but you wouldn't understand.
She died two years ago. That's all.
My friends made me place this ad.

viii.

Ache me like a bad tooth,
or a roaring ear infection,
pain beyond its source,
so that the whole world throbs
with the pulse of ragged nerve
like music, a long cry from the gut,
a love song.
Call me. I want to hear your voice.

ix.

Lovely older woman, the metallic prism of your hair, well-cut,
your smooth chin and firm calves, the pressed and tailored suits.
I want to press your soft threads, unloose the bright scarf at your throat.
You drink black coffee and read *The Washington Post.*
You wear no ring.
I'll touch your toes beneath the sheets,
and catch the moment when you sing.

x.

You, a prayer mumbled one afternoon;
me, candlesticks in paper.
You, the burnt scent of a match;
me, your intercessor.

—*Open Competition Winner*

Carrie Oeding

The Women Wear Black

even in the sun.
You wonder
if they're hip, sullen . . . oh no—hard to get?
You think they mourn
because they sleep with each other's husbands and lovers,
cover each other with gossip and glares,
raise their glasses and clink to another day
that they have spared each other, clink
to another day when they will *not* spare each other
when a man's hands tears off one woman's black.
The women are not ready to say why they wear black.
They wear black while having fun.
They know Saturday nights that are see-through, ripped, tight with fur.
They know to go to church in the morning,
but they still wear black to pray
that God is *not* a woman
and wonder how She is settling in with a heaven full of men.
The women are not ready to whisper *Amen.*
They are not ready to shout out sins.
They're too busy undressing their men.
The women are not ready to say why they wear black.

They do not know what else to dress themselves in.
But at night when they whisper to one another,
never
and never settle,
only then do they know what to wear.
But the sun rises
and heaven exists only in the light, during a day that is not theirs.
Girls, we need sunglasses.
Our squinting has blurred us into a glob of we.
How will we ever know one from another?
How can we call out naked shouts of *Delia, Mary, Bernadine?*
Women, wear black and laugh,
so I know which way to walk.
Oh, boys and men, I'm sorry,
my back turning has nothing to do with you.

—*Nominated by* Third Coast

Shann Ray

A Quiet Poem about Marital Sex

Put your fire to my forest
and pour on oil.

Your gasoline to the struck tip
of the waiting match

and I will stop whatever I'm doing
because in a minute you and I will burn down the world.

Set fire to the pipeline!
See the winter melt in less than sixty seconds,

all the wells of the glittering earth ignited
from underground at once in a thousand sites

and in a thousand cities the beacon fires on the fortified walls
say, We've won!

The gates won't wait for dawn!
They open now!

The tips of your fingers taste like oxygen
and when the torch of my tongue meets you

it's time to drop everything
and sit down quietly

and call the handyman
because

we're not worried anymore
about the bills, the yard, the work, the mess—

we're facing what's more pressing...
we've blown the doors off the house.

—Open Competition Winner

Julie Funderburk

Without Power

Another consequence of the storm:
our neighbors lost two Bradford pears,

trees that often survive just seven years
(*life of a marriage these days* was the joke),

sending up green, the tear shape
practically begging the wind.

And: for three days you and I have stayed
near each other—in the flickering meals, our talk

feeling again like secret exchange.
Tonight we wait in the city-dark;

a fallen magnolia splits the backyard.
We relax in its branches

as if we've climbed, but we've earned nothing,
running our hands along its bark

as if discovery will come: precious little,
a dim white flower, a bowl that holds

the strangeness of all I do not know of you.

—*Nominated by* The Greensboro Review

Ira Sukrungruang

In Thailand It Is Night

Today, my mother dreams of the years
she lost, standing like a river queen
on a wobbling canoe, oar digging into the murky

water of the Chaopaya, her five sisters picking
ticks from her toes. She is thirty-two
and not a nurse in a far away country, not

married to a man who loves to suck
the skin off a stewed chicken's feet, not
giving birth in the early morning,

the sun rising over a lake that roars
like an ocean. No, in her dream
she chooses which way the canoe floats.

In the distance, on the east bank,
a boy holds the sweetest mango, pulp
pale, juices running down the lengths

of his offering arms. But she drifts past,
heads for the red mountains of the north,
the place that has called to her for years.

When she wakes, she calls her only son
and tells him of her dream.
It is time to go home.

The sun has gotten too bright,
and she yearns for those hot nights
when geckos claw up screened windows,

and dogs tumble in the dusty road,
howl at the bitten moon.

—*Nominated by* Ninth Letter

Diane Kirsten Martin

Mom Poem

> "I read poetry to save time."
> —Marilyn Monroe

Mom and Marilyn

My mother and the Argentines love Marilyn,
the kitten smile, the take-me glamour.
In Buenos Aires they stand in line for hours
to get to touch the shimmering green gown
beaded with six thousand rhinestones
that Marilyn wore the night she sang
her breathy happy
birthday to Kennedy.

Mom treasures a recipe from '54—
a pineapple upside down cake—
because on the reverse of the yellowed clip
Joe DiMaggio bestows a wedding kiss
on Marilyn's inspiring lips
and on her hand, an eternity band
of thirty-five diamonds.

Mom Sets Foot in another Country

Here and here, she's not allowed,
although she can just see in,
as through the windows of a house
she once lived in, in another country

where she made coffee first thing in the morning
for sixty years, and now this thing called coffee
is bird tracks on the beach, the birds themselves
departing skyward, eroding sand.

Archaeologist, she figures
how the woman in yesterday's kitchen
would stand, where she would put
the dirt-brown dust in the pot

and where the water. How
new the world is!
She tosses out the cups and saucers
after breakfast because they are used.

Mom at Sea

Mom sits on the couch where we put her,
small boat moored on a brocade ocean.
A cloud settles; each day it covers more of her face.

Mom Comes to Me in a Dream

Naugahyde on a balsa wood frame,
face down on the carpet. It's Mom,
complaining about being left in that state.
I start over to her. Yes,
it's one of those dreams
where you need a thumb's perspective
on interstellar space.

Michelangelo's God gestures toward Adam:
There they are, on the ceiling,
fingers drawing further apart—
at arm's length, so to speak,
though face to face.

Quite the gap to spark. Time
for Noah's flood and his ark,
for the multitudes in twos, and the dove
bringing back the olive. Not godforsaken,
God help me. I sit her up. It's morning.

Mom Comes to Me from Past and Future

East on 580, south I-5 and 99, I drive
The Valley, past growers' billboards
for nuts and fruit. Twenty years from now
I will see a pistachio
and think: *My mother is dead.*

Among rows of irrigated almonds
an old Ohlone pounding acorns on a rock
looks up across centuries
to where I pass on the Interstate.

Mom Unpacked

How my arms upraised to pull back my hair
look like my mother's. How I fold
one glove into the other so they are holding hands
and tuck the tidy package in the jacket pocket
as she would do. How when Scott says,
inoperable brain cancer this afternoon
it's Mom I see announcing at the pool
that she'd an illness to trump her friends'
arthritis, hip replacements, and cardiac infarcts.
She said it the same way she'd tell you she
was first in her class in Walton Girls Latin.
Then she tripped on the beach chair
and glared at me as I helped her up.
It's the illness, I tell myself, and the next day
at Henri's buying tomatoes: *When I want tomatoes,*
I want tomatoes, grabbing the bag from me, packing
tomatoes to outlast her. *Can't you do anything?*
They would have cried if they'd been animal.

Mom Sees a Lake

What does it look like
from there, Mom? You have
no god, no taste for fiction,
no mortar to brick immortal story.
We hang on to your words,
to any indication of soaring
above this bed.

Mom Asks, Doves Assent

After a while, there's nothing to say.
Mourning doves have built a nest
in the locust at the end of the terrace
after a short courtship. You wait on your back
in the small bed of your marriage,
propped on pillows, for instructions.
How does one die?—bit by bit,
but it takes practice. Your whole life
you sharpened your pencils, did your lessons.
Good, say the doves,
good, good, good, good girl.

—*Nominated by* Nimrod

Dan Albergotti

Stones and Shadows

1. *Visiting the Stone*

The air in the car is thick and still. My father makes
a right turn through the cemetery gates, giving me
a significant look. I don't ask why. "The mausoleum
keeps expanding," he says, without irony.

"Have you ever been to a *filing?* Your mother and I
went to our first last week." I give the short laugh
that he knows well. Not funny yet again. But I see
that he's right—the mausoleum *is* expanding.

Construction materials are stacked nearby, and the frame
of an addition has been erected. The original building
is crowded. White flowers adorn its smooth stone wall
in odd spots as if they had been thrown against it

at random. We step out of the car at the back
of the graveyard, and my father leads me
to a new headstone. Then he gestures to the ten letters
cut into its face, shadows hiding in the furrows.

He tells me he likes the view and how important
that is when you think about spending eternity
in one place. Small birds stand like sentinels
on the neighboring monuments, watching us

with black pearls of eyes. Like the stone angels,
they keep us under constant vigil. Low clouds
drift by. The sound of traffic from the highway
is insufferable. I smile at my father and try

to think of kind things to say to him. He smiles.
But driving home, he is again the man I know.
"How would you like to live on Dargan Street?"
he asks with contempt as we pass the beaten houses

of the poor. "How would you like to live
in New York City?" I search for ways to interrupt,
to shut him up. But when I look left, he has become
just a voice in the driver's seat. "Son," says the voice.

"Son, I think it's going to be a good year for you."
The car arrives at the house, where my mother
is waiting, asking where we've been. She holds
the door open for us—me, the voice, my father's body.

2. Shadow

In the late afternoon, he is cooking steaks on the grill,
and we're drinking beer. The clouds have moved on.
Purple martins dart across the air, catching mosquitoes
and going in and out of their houses. We are privileged

in the extreme. And I don't want this to be a poem
of complaint. I only want to say that my father and I
are quiet. That there are words necessary and impossible,
words as grand as shadows cast by stones.

He stabs at a steak with his fork and says, "This one
is your mother's—she doesn't want any blood in hers.
She wants it about as well done as done can be."
My mother's in the kitchen, cooking the potatoes.

The shadows of the martins swim in the grass.
The shadows of the grass dig into the earth.
The shadows of the earth carve the moon
into crescents, halves, and empty holes.

I notice that the sundial in the plant bed is not
positioned well. "Your sundial is keeping bad time,"
I tell my father. He smiles and says, "That's not
what I got it for," pointing to the image in relief,

old man with scythe, and the quotation: "Grow old
along with me, the best is yet to be." Impossible,
grand. The earth is beneath us. The birds watch us.
The blade's shadow quietly cuts X from I.

—*Open Competition Winner*

Duffie Taylor

Why Does Beauty Have an Arch?

I have asked this twice.
Why does beauty have an arch?
Do you not agree; do you not believe
Beauty, too, is structural?

Dalloway is walking home, his arms full
Of roses; at this moment, they are red,
And he will say those words to his wife;
It was the silks; it was the scissors.

And it is beautiful, should we doubt it,
If, suppose, the roses were yellow?
Really, beauty is factual, it builds upon
Those very things one forgets in the end.

Where on earth will you mistake a sugar beet
For Jack Johnsons, coal boxes, whizz-bangs;
This is the dump; it is ploughing season.
Still, occasionally, an officer dies.

The Somme is a slow-moving river
Winding through a peat-bottomed valley
Below beech woods; partridge and hares;
Clay-smeared beet; *tir de barrage;* dud shells;
Globes and cones; November; weeds.

Dalloway has come home; the words built up.
This is a world of perfect order (as the poem follows).
At one time, flowers had overgrown the parapets
Of trenches. It is beautiful now.

—Nominated by Hollins University

Jennifer Chang

Conversation with Owl and Clouds

Owl-night, moon-gone, my wherewithal
is yellow pine. Is trillium and unfurled frond.

Clouds—a cantilever of the trees, vapor-
plied architecture of the ephemeral—teach me

the apparition-life, what tunes the branches'
nocturne off-key: how do bodies turn into

song? Glow of dust and sandstone light, stars
dropped like pebbles, like crumbs, heretofore

a fairy tale trail. Barn owl, secretive and out-
spoken, you spout two minds, a hiding place

and a traffic sign. What's this absence
you speak of? Nonsense-yakking *lost soul,*

lost soul, the self-question that grows—
Who what?—odd and old.

Build me up into the fog, into brevity
made beautiful, the wet-dressed disaster

that's rain, that's the storm-threat of forest fire.
I want to be ornate and ornery. More than

a vapor-child, a night's ward like the white
monkshood tucking under its bud, too shameful

to flower. I am hearing it: spring's first wild melt,
each drop trickling into the next, a minor

chord. So snow's gone, so how can I be
ice dissolving in water?

Cloud me, sparrowing and bark-loose,
each season's dark ambition: a patient pattern

gone. O, I am hearing it: this say-nothing
noise, how the world's clamor-born and

sorrowful, tricked for loss, the silent purpling
of crocuses mouthing back at the owl:

I will not, and soon—

—Nominated by The Asian American Writers' Workshop

Andrew Kozma

Too Steep to Climb

In the air the still distant and uproarious smoke
scaling the dark rungs of trees to unwind
into twists of small shadow eaten by the clouds.
The crematorium is just one thin spoke

of ritual holding us at bay, and what a kind
dictator to present death only as a shroud.
Forgive me, father, for I have missed
your skin, your eyes, I have been blind

to your absence. Sometimes as I've drowsed
an insistent voice (I've called it yours) has kissed
my ears ungently and scoured me from sleep
hungry for more. We were left a crowd

of ashes and bone. I've tried to make a list
of what was lost. I want to say however much I keep.
Take this one answer: life is the dawn and our souls,
if that is who we are, are burned from the earth like mist.

Be comforted. There is no grave so deep
it does not fold again into a mountain.

—Open Competition Winner

Paula Bohince

The Fly

Did I invite him with thoughts of sugar?
All day he chased me, trailing
blue dashes, settling in the hot tent of my ear
as a nomad and medium
whose psychic abilities outmatched my own
so I assumed, all afternoon, his mind—
the absolute pleasures of warm flesh,
of washing, balanced on the rippling drum . . .
There was no room for remembering
a youth that seemed to fall away in minutes,
no space for regret, only a pledge to live
intensely, hovering inches above the body.

——Open Competition Winner

Eleanor Stanford

Darwin in the Cape Verde Islands

I.

In the market, a woman grabs my arm
to sell me unfamiliar fruits. I hold an apple
in my palm no bigger than a peach stone.
My money has no value here. Take
my cufflinks: they are useless
as a pair of dung beetles, silver exoskeletons
glinting in my outstretched hand.

A man can't trust his senses.
The clarity that draws the hills in sharp relief
is nothing like the clarity
of home. Young girls in bright shawls
flutter like a circle of doves, winged palms
beating time on their thighs. What instrument
can measure this aerial transparency? Not
the hygrometer; not the swift pulse
of blood, the needle of my compass, quivering.

II.

It's a delirium, this haze that descends
westward from the continent. How
to judge this happiness that descends
in a fine silt upon one's shoulders? How
to echo the sparse beauty, the lava fields
a single sprig of green would spoil?
If indeed, a person who's seen fields
of lavender on the horizon, the spoils
of too long away from land, can judge.
In the market, a slab of tuna fresh from sea
rests on a woman's head. Its flesh is judge
of what the day will yield: a placid sea,
pink-bellied sky. Who that has just walked
for the first time in a grove of cocoa-nuts
will question that a fish as well has walked
on two legs from the sea? The cocoa-nuts
rattle in the wind, and shake the dust
from their sharp fronds; his own happiness
flutters like a compass. How to shake the dust
from this strange body, to own this happiness?

III.

Dear Reader, for what novel aspects have we scoured
the globe, only to long for our own gardens, sour
cherries and seckle pears, the orderly rows
of thyme and marigolds? Still, everything grows
from something else, and these plots we mind tend

toward propagation. The missives that I send
will find my wife knitting by the fireside.
Does she undo her stitches every night,
while I lose my own steps in this dust?
At the old church, colored flags flutter
and an ancient priest mumbles blessings
in strange Portuguese. Outside, the wind threshing
the banana leaves repeats itself. But, Reader, dear,
the final page remains unwritten here:
This earth offers no certainty for cows or goats
or the acacias in their dusty coats, growth
stunted by the trade winds. The fine dust broke
our instruments; it gathers on the masthead, chokes
the sun. It comes from Africa; and why
should this surprise? We have traveled farther, blind
to what has brought us here. Leave India, its teas
and silks and spices, to others. The tree
of knowledge grows in more barren climes;
all I seek is this: a way to unwind time,
to trace the story to its roots. The women,
black as jet, watch us with their inky
eyes. What secrets do they weave into the bright
cloths they tie about their hips? They hide
intention in a blur of dance. The youngest girls
know how to move like that, how to twirl
their bodies to the frantic song. These islands
breed an instinct for survival: the silent
lizards with their darting tongues and bulging
eyes; the cuttle-fish, chameleon-like, divulging
nothing but a blur of ink in its wake.

It's a rare species of happiness that takes
here. Reader, it confounds my science;
if it has a name, perhaps it's *transience.*

—Nominated by The University of Virginia

Carrie Jerrell

When the Rider Is Truth

I am froth and lather, sent steaming
through jade fields while he sits
heavy in the saddle, beating love songs
on my flanks I'm slow to learn.
His snapped whip rings like church bells.
He prays my name. In different winds,
it rhymes with *win* and *race*. At night,
he rests against my neck and tells me
stars are born between my heartbeats,
though they're unreachable this trip.
Still, with him I feel sure-footed
running on this soil of sand,
this miraculous green,
where every day is like no other
in its symmetry of hill and valley.
When shadows blend, I want the blinders on.
I want the spurs and speed. It's then
I understand tight reins, a firm grip,
the bitter iron on my tongue,
the blood and sharper bit I'm driven with.

—*Nominated by* 32 Poems

Damon McLaughlin

Ceremony

If I were taking lives, I would take hands
first, parting the bones of the wrist with one
good snap, and they'd pop off
like spent hibiscus buds, the fingers
and the palms collapsed like paper cups
no mouth has touched in years. I would

palm each palm, opening the hand
little finger first, slowly,
as though talking down a fist.

And then I'd pry the thumb,
that fleshy horse, to stroke its velvet nose
so soft it's silk, it's air, a ghost touched and rising
from the sheet that binds it to the world

the way these lines traverse the hand
mapping heart and love and life and how
we will hold on to such promises

though they spin like leaves all around us
and dodge the grips of scientists and priests
who held them in their bibles,

and the blues man's fingertips, cuticles
picked at by guitar strings, calluses hard
as the mechanic's or the farmer's
whose hands swell with years of milking,
of laying the fence that binds him to the land

and one to another, earth, sea, and sky.
I would hold up these hands and pray for rain.
I would hold them up like bowls and fonts,
like reservoirs the clouds have filled
for us to swim in, to lose, to find ourselves.
I would offer them like flowers for the living
and the dead, for the handful of earth between.

—*Open Competition Winner*

Tama Baldwin

Bad Weather

Hope is as absurd as
delphinium springing
from a crust of snow, blue
flowers born of the blue hued
suffocation of ice.
Hope is as ridiculous as rain
becoming dimes or diamonds or
kisses or God's tears.
It is as impossible as
rearranging the galaxy—
making many earths to use—
the cosmic clock nothing but a disc
under the dj's hand, time shoved back
becoming a backbeat, a groove
we can dance to: you're younger / you're
older / you're younger / you're
really rocking now—shake it baby, shake your—Wait!
You move your body. That's it, isn't it—?
Hope is a hop you once upon a time
freely gave, in a game—or for no
reason at all. I remember

boogying in the vegetable aisle,
dancing with my sisters,
singing *heard it through the grapevine*—refusing
our mother's tears, the war
outside the grocery store doors,
the meanness and catastrophe
waiting for us all.

—*Nominated by* Poetry International

Daniel Groves

A Stranger Here Myself

> *…that benighted city.*
> —Frank Lloyd Wright

"*She's a brick…* (and one and two and) *…house.*"
Funk follows formstone out of vacant blocks
where row on row of more brick houses drowse
in sprawling shade, as the last carthorse click-clocks
in time toward when, her ships come in, the docks
were bustling—*swart, side-burned, the common boors
unloaded wares for Clipper commodores…*

Loaded nowheres; the Broadway (too broad, indeed)
of memory, yoking past and present—witty
or cavalier—to fail what we succeed
(hard fact, brick factory in complicity
with dream, our unincorporated city,
Retropolis). Though where but this co-here
could all our incoherencies cohere?

Such as the concrete underneath my feet
and abstraction of the signs above my head

(downtown and up—both are a one-way street,
but parallel), ST. PAUL and CHARLES. Misled,
perhaps, by mere book smarts, too many dead
white males, my do-it-yourselfer projects upon
historic structures, fallen, nearly gone,

the will to restoration—which, of course,
must mean conversion, too, so that the former
fills a function (cart behind the horse).
That old-line statesman, gentlemanly farmer
Lord Baltimore could not provide for more
than meets the idling idealist today
of his Jacobite angel-wrestling, on display

through centuries (like Greek Town, Druid Hill;
the masquerading *Bromo-Seltzer* tower,
Domino's Sugar; Pig Town, Butcher's Hill;
boarded-up storefront churches, 24-hour
Rite-Aid; Beth Steel, LaCrosse; a higher power,
up with *The Sun* clock-punching; rhyme, meter;
Lyric Opera House, Mechanic Theater).

But this is horseplay, hackwork—arm in arm,
these couples make a scene that made out worse
as, from "The Monumental" into "Charm"
city went Baltimore. By some perverse
horror, or pragmatism, Poe and Peirce
died poor, dispersed, as Mencken's burboisie,
(ever-mercurial) sounded-off Key,

with coltish *unitas,* unto the local
heavens (blue horseshoe collar, aureole
of looming lights) for Weaver and, lo, Cal
before they took the field at Memorial
away, and picked its carcass clean. Its soul?
Nevermore? The ravings carry on;
no bardic songbird, only carrion,

I join in the lost cause, beat a dead horse,
drink at The Hippo (if not Hippocrene)—
my (equi)vocation, mixing metaphors
for this Metapolis, moving between
READ and CHASE (at EAGER, epicene
epicenter) and backward—significantly?—
since age eighteen, from UNIVERSITY.

My twenties in the Thirties—classic white
marble stoops to conquer, an attic room.
But thirties in the Twenties? Forties—wait,
I-40? The Inner Harbor's recovered womb?
Through netherhoods of dome and spire, doom
and aspiration, what prestigial
detail remains of our original

old glory, grandeur? Is charm a monument?
The antiquated anti-quaint? The odd
wrought-iron frontispiece on Space for Rent,
the odd wrought-iron star on the façade,
remember, bears a load (but household god
gargoyles' stone-faced perseverance is
only to keep up disappearances).

Form follows function—will, that is, outlive
its use. Still, fretwork, grating, colored pane
and painted screen, fancy, if useless, give
perspective. Elaborate frames that show their strain
(the crack, the pipes); the imminent domain
of fixer-uppers—junk supplies our fix:
the *ton* of bric-a-brac, or the ton of bricks.

Will building blocks that, layer on layer (bored,
martyred, mortar-boarded), we pre-cast to spell,
from TIME and LABOR, BALTIMORE, be floored,
dropping, again, to BLAME and RIOT? Well,
one noticed, visiting, in those who dwell
in this *De trop*olis, "an inverse pride
in not being noticed." Suicide,

like immortality, would draw too much
attention. The *National Bohemian*
natty beau fades out, with no retouch,
winking conspiratorially, man-to-man.
Suspenders, dandy moustache, frothy can—
each trademark property, condemned, persists
for fetishists and counterfeitishists,

stung with nostalgia by some buzzword ("Hon"),
by beehive sentimentality, sickly sweet,
glazed over, overdone, over and done,
done over. My baroque-ial school aesthete
keeps the faith, invokes the Absolute,
the cataclysm, the holy trivia quiz
"as it was in the beginning, shall be, is,

without end." Greek Revival; Drag Queen Anne;
Flamboyant Gothic; Georgian; French Chateau;
Carthorse; Iron Horse; the Iron Man;
cart-blanche; wrought irony; my B&O
roundhouse, where trains of thought, however slow,
are linked-up to a one-track mind to run,
always on time, birth to oblivion,

Golden, Gilded, Gelded Ages hence . . .
into the turn, the backstretch, comes the night-
mare, my paling dark-horse, with a sense
of show, and place, and loss, to find daylight
across this bay to which I have not quite
been brought up yet (the racing form, the poem,
and I, perfunctorily, follow), head for home.

—Nominated by The Sewanee Writers' Conference

Amber Dawn

How I Got My Tattoo

Every other weekend I ate green olives, crude slices of cheddar, ritz crackers, smoked
sardines straight from the can with the turn-key lid, garlic pickles and pepperoni
dipped in sour cream, spring onions, and hard boiled eggs rolled under my father

's palm until the shell fell away like lizard skins then rolled again
in a mound of kosher salt because these were the foods that coalesce
with father's recent divorce status and with gin. When

I hit my girlfriend, Valentine, with the phone receiver (a decade
later) I was dead set on having green olives as the complimentary topping
on our delivery pizza. She wanted green peppers and bellyached

about how we stopped eating vegetables and going for our all-night walks.
We only walked those walks, I reminded her, for the city to become field, or empty
parking lot, or a stretch of quiet railroad where we could kiss each other raw
and scream and hide from Burgard Vocational High School and god and

daylight. Cocaine
is turning you into a fucking asshole, she said and picked olives from her
half of the pizza to feed them to me; a few missed my mouth and rolled inside
my shirt and onto the gold and denim blue floral sofa, where we slept, a mess
of limbs and unconscious youth. I never lost

my appetite as an addict. I'm glad I was a girl and there were horse races
and truck stops and twenty-four-hour diners where a girl, with a bit of glitter
lip gloss, could count on the done-with-their-day men, up-or-down-on-their-luck
men, ball-busted broken-backed men, plain-sick-of-spending-time-with-other-
men men to offer a grilled cheese sandwich so I didn't have to raid the dumpster

behind the Nabisco factory with Petey and Steve. They always smelled like corn syrup.
Petey had beautiful eyelashes that hid the bloodshot like burlesque dancer
's feather fans. I would have let him touch me but his hands were the kind
of filthy that won't scrub clean. I wish I could say I've been clean

since the day Valentine died. I was living in an artist loft where I made non
-wearable ball gowns out of copper wire, old costume jewelry and crayfish
claws I had saved up over the years and spray painted gold.
My girlfriend at the time, Jesse, was kind and always lied
when I asked her if my art stank like fish; she had her arms around
me before I even hung up the phone. Valentine's little sister told me I was
the only one she would call, me and 911, because it was just too awful.
I returned to my old dealer's house with the confederate flag hung in the bay
window and the stupid smoke that couldn't find its way out
of the living room and I told everyone there
Valentine had overdosed in her sister's bathroom and the funeral would be on Wednesday
at Our Lady of Perpetual Forgiveness church. My skin itched
from the second-hand freebased coke and I had to go home and take seventeen
Gravol because that is all we had in the medicine cabinet and I wanted to sleep
for as many days as humanly possible
but Jesse made me walk
in circles around the coffee
table for hours
before she was sure

I wouldn't pass out.
I quit

for good up north in a small village where my hosts brought down a deer,
which I volunteered to help them skin and piece the meat. I didn't expect
the animal to resist the knife the way it did. Everyone was amused at how I struggled
with its heavy leg in my lace-trimmed summer dress, they said they had never seen a white
girl so willing to get blood on her hands since their land was taken. The children made
up words and told me they where Indian words long forgotten, then squealed hysterically
when I tried to use these words in a sentence. I guess, without realizing it,

I enjoyed being an outsider. Sure, I've traveled and gotten the kind of attention a girl
gets when she is traveling alone. The tattoo on my back has been a means for men
(and some women) to initiate conversation or touch, poking at the raised ink peeking out
of my shirt collar. Hiro approached me in a park

in Osaka while I was trying to coax a stray dog to let me pet him and asked me to come
for karaoke and drinks. I ordered cream soda that surprised me by being emerald green.
The cartoonish rendition of Valentine, her half
-winking eye, her leopard print swim suit,

her halo that was supposed to be gold but I got too sore for the tattooist
to finish her color made Hiro ask, why did you get this tattoo?

I told him to kiss Valentine's lips, my shoulder, and we sang Beatles songs: "I feel
the ice is slowly melting, little darling, it seems like years since it's been clear."

—Nominated by The University of British Columbia

Michael Meinhardt

Honor amongst Thieves

Jewel heists are less complicated, say, than love affairs.
                                        Integral calculus.
        Put your ear flush to the vault door, maybe crack your fingers,   locking them
and stretching inside out.
                        Hold your breath. Turn the tumbler, click-clocking beneath ferric skin.
        This is not one of those modern, electronic models
                                with laser lighting and motion detectors.
        A spinner: Ambivalent and ambidextrous.
        A secret keeper in small company,
                                already knows she is meant to lose.

Some thieves are just
                quicker than others.
                                Touch her. Just the right way.
        Shut your mouth and listen to her.
                She will tell you everything,
                                make things up, once the truth is spent.
Just to keep you there.

If you listen closely, the sadness may surface.

       Not so much a whimper

  As the sigh of a recently opened door,

         now that she has so much more to say,

   and no one left to hear it.

            —Open Competition Winner

Steve Mueske

On Poetics

If, under the aegis of dead men,
you see obsolescence, celebrate
the gas's cold compression in the balloon. If

the experiment fails, you may have to start near
the middle,
in the nursery of opinions.

Don't talk about the sky, for it is older
than conversation. Likewise the heart, thrashing in the ship's futtocks.
These are commercials for the moon.

In time—

the stars, chattering in the standing room, will stop grieving
for their sheen;
snakes will abandon their sexual terrorism;
wine will return
to a constellation of grapes.

I'm waiting in the pub, watching the dust sing madly
in the weighted light,
a latecomer to the ballyhoo.

—Open Competition Winner

Dave Lucas

Epithalamium

After they each had landed in divorce,
my parents met each other in a bar—
the Robin Hood, off Euclid. Unpopular
and dark (the teachers' after-school resource),
just right for a mutual friend to introduce
David and Barb. A Chardonnay, a beer.
A smile and laugh. I am that second's scar.
Next August they were married, on a course
to Dad's dominion of the couch and grill,
Mom in the kitchen, separate and severe.
So strange to envy this, their singling of plurals:
the drowsy, boring breaking of the fever
I burn with, as I wait in bars for girls
I may or may not care about forever.

—Open Competition Winner

Lisa Gluskin

Jars

These last weeks, so many
       things, just so much and all the mason jars
          filling up with light and oddments, lids off

for everything rolling around in there:
       car and computer crashes (minor), your twisted ankle,
          a marriage (ours), trail of ants swirling

down into the cat dish, basil and dandelions
       leaping up in the yard: What did I think
          would happen? We were transformed,

and obstinate. The phone kept ringing. A bruise
       on my thigh from the suitcase, another
          mid-forearm, shape of a thumb

in brown and blue. New sheets
       on the neighbor's line. I paid bills, juggled
          money and packages. Could not stop

smiling, shivering all at once. Yesterday
          someone left a ring of soft blue pebbles
                    on the front steps, where the bus pauses

on its way to the beach. I took out the trash,
          took a call from a friend (her mother's throat
                    ringed with tumor). Back in bed, shivering,

then the morning, held down and arching
          toward you. Three jars on the dresser:
                    tulips, water, ash.

—Open Competition Winner

Sandra Beasley

After Miscarriage

Each morning her husband rides his mower across the lawn,
then back again. Each night he runs his hand aground
on the helpless bank of her belly.

She knows they expect needles, knives, firehot brands.
They need her to own the cinders, a hole
that can burn itself clean away.

How, then, to explain that for weeks her girl had been
a trout, a nesting of cool bones and pale flesh
sewn to the bottom of a muddy river?

She compliments the peach cobbler. She feels.
She does. And she has always known her fingers to be a net
she could not lace tight enough.

—Nominated by American University

Cynthia Marie Hoffman

Dear Alexander Nevsky,

Do you know what things they've said
about you since you died at Gorodets?
They say as you lay in the open
casket, your fist uncurled like a morning glory.
This alone is no call for alarm;
it's a common thing for cadavers
to interrupt their own autopsy
by sitting up and spilling the heart and spleen
into their laps. But legend has it
your palm clasped shut again
when the scroll, on which your burial prayer
was written, was laid in it. They made you a saint
and granted you a street for this,
the longest and widest in Petersburg.

It's from here that I write you this letter, admitting
I've walked the Nevsky Prospekt for seven days
and haven't thought about you once, until now.
I'm not ashamed to say it. Instead,
I've only thought of Akhmatova, how she
too walked here, how down from the Fontanka

she dragged her sullen profile on the palace wall,
nose like a broken wing. I believe in the poet
who sits in a chair worn through to the springs,
who stands at Kresty prison with an arm full of bread,
who always packs her nitroglycerin tablets in her purse
and dies anyway.
Nevsky, namesake of asphalt, saint
of the timely convulsion, pray for me.

—*Nominated by* Phoebe

Matthew Hittinger

The Fresco Worker Appears Suddenly in the Picture

When he rubs his hands for blood flow it snows.
If I were a leper, if I were a snake . . . Shavings skim

the fresco's surface as strips separate, peel, palm
creases deepened. *. . . would I cease to hold these hands*

together, would I slough, erase my face . . . Slick slate
bodies of fish spread wing-fins, swim and leap

across the wall to form an ellipse: they mirror
the fresco worker's face as his thumb goads metal,

scales polished in circles. *Skin becomes scale.* Lime
and granite kneaded to the consistency of dough

transform him. *I am a leper—no, a snake that sloughs
itself to reveal that supple layer.* If he were a leper,

like a leper, would the swirls and lines deepen,
separate, cease to hold carpals to wrist to radius?

If he were the snake, like a snake, at least the lines
would stretch, hold, redden into pink scars. Either

way he sheds skin, rubs olive oil over fingertips,
the metal tool, the wall; his eyes grow as distant

as the eyes of the fish. He breathes, skin passes
over gills, leaves yellow wings slippery, reflection

born as he swims, slick-skinned, *I am land-scape*,
shadow on marble, shadow on grit, *I am fish*.

—Nominated by Memorius

Cecily Parks

Self-Portrait as Angler's Damselfly

It takes a certain type to be devoured
daily, to slide into each fish's jaw

with no song in my throat. Please consider,
in big-river country, the allure

of the miniature, of tinsel, feather and thread,
of stiff, glittering hackles and glued wings—

and know when the mouth strikes, I'm barb and hook
and bound by filament to bony ground.

Show me a safer way to want.
Existing in repetition is not so far

from living in ritual, where consolation
outweighs consequence and all trajectories

bend toward the center. Darling, there will never
be more than the arc I describe, the flash

of a trout turning beneath me to feed, a briefest
darkness. This landscape allows no hiding—

a thundercloud is visible for miles
and no amount of silt can cloak a current's

appetite—the trick is to prohibit
hunger, which is not far from expectation.

—*Nominated by* The Virginia Quarterly Review

Laura-Gray Street

Ring-Necks

Three hours she avoids the cock
and hen, flushed from the same rise, tucked
close as sleeping lovers, a delicacy

too touching to waste. Still the driveway
stays empty. Shushing the whimper
of the dog's linoleum-clicking dreams,

she lifts each bird by the neck and turns
to his penciled instructions. He'll have
some explaining to do. But no use

crying as blood jewels their beaks.
The quills she tugs sputter
like candles. Down drifts,

and the dog rouses its nose
to the smoky air. How brightly
wings snap at the shoulder, span

and retract. Flesh and breastbone
yield to knife-slice a handful
of curled intestines, plump

stomach, thumbpads of liver.
Flushed under tap the parsed guts
quiver; run clear. She plumbs

the cavity again, feels how firmly
the small heart roots before it gives
over to its leaded end.

She crouches; offers it on the flat
of her hand, the dog's warm tongue
sponging her open palm. That

moment she notes the presence of another,
smooth, indecipherable as a creek stone
—then it's gone.

—*Nominated by* Blackbird

Jennifer Chapis

After Ovarian Surgery

She dines on blueberries in the bath.
Each slow berry a moment slipping.
Blue storm, rain-sounds. Her body is all steam,
velvet, snow—millions of minuscule air
bubbles cling, and wipe away like shaving
cream in thick stripes. Nothing holds the eye

like the skin of a woman. Her gray eyes
shift from bath to ceiling to bath.
She imagines a baker shaving
the fur from a peach, the fruit slips
from his knife, and his heart leaks like an air
mattress. The knot of him inside her. Steam

risen from a pastry, vanilla light. Its steamy
core silent, the hunter's lion eyes
its own rupture. Infinite. In mid-air.
I almost vanished. Red crawls about the bath.
Her insides are nothing, but an itch. She slips
a bathing cap over her hair, and sinks. Seconds shave

by.   *Breathe!*   Petal-like soap shavings
slide over her thighs, the pubis thick with steam,
and the incisions below the hips where a slip
might hang. The navel—a berry, an eye
looking in. (Keep the incisions dry. Bathe
them in Bacitracin, vitamin E, let the air

nurse them.) She's near-met death before: in a hot air
balloon dragged by a shifting wind-stream—shaving
past a net of electrical wires. And in the bath
as a child. In this stolen porcelain dish, the steam
sighs. It penetrates and undoes. . . . What owns the eyes
like this?—a woman dreaming cerulean, slipping

berries onto her tongue. Each one slips
furtively inside, her warmest self ajar. By air
and sea they travel the body. The berry an eye-
witness to the scores of wants untouched. (Shave
the brain. Love the infant unconceived.) Oh, steamy
berry, delicious sapphire, this jewel bath

red, blue—*My lion's heart slipped out, sunk and shaved.*
You are the air itself, and I a mother underwater. Steam-
opened morning glory, eye of this rich rich bath.

—Open Competition Winner

Clay Matthews

Scissors

The radio cracked and buzzed,
the Rolling Stones singing Let's
spend the night together while I

pulled leaves from your hair
and burned them with matches
one by one until my fingers

were black and the air smelled
like a Saturday with football on
in the background. You looked

at the eve of the roof and the Chrysler's
flat tire and not me and for that
I felt like a photograph in the background

of some black-and-white film, the *en*
of the *mis-en-scene* if you will,
or won't, it doesn't much matter

either way. Harry said something
once about how we were like two peas
in a pod, and I agreed, except for

there being more than two peas
in a pod. Once you smelt like the river
and for that I loved you. Once you

tasted like canned soup and for that
I wanted a bigger spoon. The radio
buzzed again and I played with the hanger

that masqueraded as an antennae.
I have masqueraded as a cold pillow
and slippers by the bedroom door.

I have worn white sheets and acted
as a ghost when you walked into the house.
Every time I watch a good movie now

I look in the mirror and think about
changing my hair. I'd let you cut it, if you
asked. I'd let you turn me into something

handsome, dark, and tall.

—Open Competition Winner

Allen Braden

First Elk, 1939

There's Al Knoll and O. L. Hesner next to the carcass,
my father at eighteen and Uncle Tillman farther off.
Julian Sommers too, out of place in a raccoon coat
more accurate for downtown's Post Alley
than somewhere above Devil's Table in the Cascades.
This bull elk they bugled into range then fixed to the hood
of a Model A coupe was what the camera's lens
had brought into focus and kept whole for over sixty years:
the seven-point rack not yet hacksawed off
to adorn the bunkhouse back home in the valley;
the four quarters, the haunches and shoulders, not yet stripped,
soaked in a barrel of brine and cured for winter;
the prized teeth not yet gentled out of the jawbone
to pretty the watch chain of any pinstriped Mason.
Some, my father says, seem meant for slaughter,
for nothing but a slug in the head and a throat slit
to drain gallons of blood from the ready meat.
The occasion scrawled upon the picture frame is certain.
Otherwise the war would have revised the scene:
Tillman and Hesner on tour in the South Pacific,
uncertain whether only they were meant for beaches

strewn with shrapnel, wreckage, and billowing smoke.
My father is, after all, no bigger than my thumb,
no more noteworthy than any of the others
except the camera captured the likeness,
for a moment, of the man he would become.

—*Nominated by* The Virginia Quarterly Review

Carol Ann Davis

Distal

As I walk along St. Philips, the dusk fills my lungs
and the bells of six o'clock make tiny equations
in the air. On my corner
the lights of the church set it on fire,
the houses surround in a kind of kneel.

Where's Fra Angelico now? I've wanted to lick the walls
of his frescoes and taste watercolor ribs.
I've wanted to eat off blue flow
before the machine made lines so precise

the ceramic no longer gave. If I am still,
things around me move back a little in their tracks,
but not far enough. It will be hard to see it

when my own heart
drops into my hand like a fish.
It will be hard to be done seeing.

—*Nominated by* The Southern Review

Hailey Leithauser

The Moon Speaks of Alzheimer's

When it comes at last, it is everything
you had hoped for.
The days smaller and darker,

the minutes longer and less
involved. What
is the difference of one face

from another?
What is the use of a hand?
Fields fill with rain

and rain becomes a silencing
of silence.
Oh Oh Oh, you say

looking out the window,
how the clouds are lovely,
how the grass is green.

—*Nominated by* The Antioch Review

Contributors' Notes

KRISTIN ABRAHAM is pursuing her M.F.A. in creative writing at West Virginia University. Her poetry and essays have appeared or are forthcoming in *can we have our ball back?*, *Rio: A Journal of the Arts*, *Delmar*, *Elixir*, *Harpur Palate*, *Phoebe*, and *Ghost of a Chance*.

DAN ALBERGOTTI's poems have appeared in *Ascent*, *Meridian*, *Mid-American Review*, *New Orleans Review*, *Prairie Schooner*, *The Virginia Quarterly Review*, and other journals. He was a Tennessee Williams Scholar at the 2003 Sewanee Writers' Conference, a fellow at the Virginia Center for the Creative Arts in July 2004, and the Richard Soref Scholar in Poetry at the 2004 Bread Loaf Writers' Conference. A graduate of the M.F.A. program at UNC Greensboro and former poetry editor of *The Greensboro Review*, he currently serves as associate poetry editor of *storySouth* and teaches at Coastal Carolina University.

BETH BACHMANN's recent poems appear in *The Southern Review*, *Antioch*, *Image*, and elsewhere; new work is forthcoming in *Prairie Schooner* and *Blackbird*. A graduate of the Johns Hopkins M.A. Program, she teaches creative writing at Vanderbilt University.

TAMA BALDWIN's poems have appeared in *The Massachusetts Review*, *Gulf Coast*, *Green Mountains Review*, *Poetry International*, *Folio*, *Notre Dame Review*, *Many Mountains Moving*, *Ms.*, *The Georgia Review*, *Poetry*, and others.

VALERIE BANDURA's poems have appeared in *Cimarron Review*, *The Greensboro Review*, *Crazyhorse*, *Hubbub*, and others, and are forthcoming in *Poet Lore* and a Russian-

American anthology edited by Anya Silver. She is currently the Joan Beebe Teaching Fellow at Warren Wilson College in Swannanoa, North Carolina.

SANDRA BEASLEY lives in Washington, D.C. and her poems have appeared or are forthcoming in *Rosebud, Dogwood, Gargoyle, Cimarron Review, Reed, Rhino, The Baltimore Review, Texas Poetry Journal, Three Candles,* and *Passages North.* Her manuscript, *Materfamilias,* was a finalist for the 2004 Kore Press First Book Prize, and she has held fellowships to the Indiana University Writer's Conference, Vermont Studio Center, and the Virginia Center for Creative Arts.

PAULA BOHINCE's manuscript, *Charity,* was selected as a readers' runner-up for the 2005 Yale Younger Poets Prize. Her poems have recently appeared or are forthcoming in *AGNI, Alaska Quarterly Review, Shenandoah, Sou'wester, Mississippi Review, Mid-American Review,* and elsewhere. She's been a resident at the MacDowell Colony, the recipient of an artist's grant from the Puffin Foundation, and a semifinalist for the Discovery/*The Nation* Prize. She teaches at the New School and Montclair State University.

ALLEN BRADEN has received a 2005 National Endowment for the Arts fellowship, an Artist Trust grant, the *Witness* Emerging Writer Prize, and the Grolier Poetry Prize. He has published in *The New Republic, The Virginia Quarterly Review, Colorado Review, Shenandoah, The Southern Review, The Threepenny Review, Meridian,* and elsewhere.

BRIAN BRODEUR received an M.F.A. from George Mason University in August 2005. Recent work has appeared or is forthcoming in *New Orleans Review, Meridian, Pleiades, Crab Orchard Review, Smartish Pace,* and *The Gettysburg Review.*

JENNIFER CHANG's poems have appeared or are forthcoming in *Barrow Street, Gulf Coast, New England Review, Pleiades, The Virginia Quarterly Review,* and *Asian American Poetry: The Next Generation.* The title poem of her manuscript *The History of Anonymity* received the 2004 Campbell Corner Poetry Prize. She is the 2005 Van

Lier Fellow in Poetry at the Asian American Writers' Workshop and was awarded the Louis Untermeyer scholarship to the 2005 Bread Loaf Writers' Conference. She teaches in the creative writing program at Rutgers University.

JENNIFER CHAPIS was awarded first place in *The GSU Review*'s 2005 annual poetry contest judged by Thomas Lux and is the winner of *The Florida Review*'s 2005 Editor's Prize. She has recently published poems with *Barrow Street, Hayden's Ferry Review, McSweeney's, Minnesota Review, Phoebe, Quarterly West*, and *Spoon River Poetry Review*, among others. Previously on New York University's award-winning faculty, Jennifer operates the Web site design and online marketing company, WebAha!, www.webaha.com, and is an editor with Nightboat Books, www.nightboat.org.

GARY JOSEPH COHEN's poems have or will appear in *Isotope, New Orleans Review, Euphony, CutBank, Heliotrope, Spinning Jenny, Antietam Review, The Berkshire Review, Writing the River Anthology*, and elsewhere. In the spring of 2003, Cohen served as The Badlands National Park Poet-in-Residence, and was featured on South Dakota Public Radio's *Arts Report* with host Susan Hanson. Cohen lives in Manhattan with his wife, Rebecca, and teaches media arts at The Calhoun School.

TEMPLE CONE is an assistant professor of English at the United States Naval Academy. His first chapbook, *Considerations of Earth and Sky*, was published in 2005 by Parallel Press. His poems have won awards including the John Lehman Award in Poetry from *Wisconsin Quarterly Review*, an Academy of American Poets Award, and an Honorable Mention for the Tor House Poetry Prize; his poems have appeared in many journals, including *Southern Humanities Review, Southern Poetry Review, Green Mountains Review, North Dakota Quarterly*, and *Midwest Quarterly*. He lives in Annapolis, Maryland with his wife and daughter.

RANDALL COUCH teaches poetry and poetics at Arcadia University and serves on the planning committee of Penn's Kelly Writers House. He received a Pennsylvania Council on the Arts fellowship in poetry in 2000 and graduated in 2003 from the Warren Wilson College M.F.A. Program for Writers.

JUDITH COX's awards include a 2003 residency fellowship from the Virginia Center for the Creative Arts, a 2003 residency from Fundación Valparaíso, and the 2000 Thomas Wolfe Fiction Prize. Her stories have appeared in magazines and journals, including *The Mississippi Review, The American Literary Review, The Village Rambler, Parting Gifts, Potomac Review,* and *Snake Nation Review,* and numerous anthologies. She has taught fiction at the Writers' Center at the Chautauqua Institution, the Danville Writer's Conference, and at the Writers' Center in Bethesda, Maryland.

CAROL ANN DAVIS's first book, *Feast Day Elegy,* is forthcoming from Tupelo Press. Her work has appeared in recent issues of *AGNI, The Southern Review,* and *The Threepenny Review.* She teaches creative writing at The College of Charleston, where she is assistant professor and editor of *Crazyhorse.*

AMBER DAWN is an M.F.A. student in creative writing at the University of British Columbia. Her poems have been published in several Canadian literary journals, including *Fireweed, Event,* and *Dandelion.* For three years she has co-organized and curated events at Crash Vancouver's Indie Writers' Fest. She is a coeditor of and a contributor in the anthology *With A Rough Tongue* (Arsenal Pulp Press, 2005).

JULIE FUNDERBURK has poems in *Ploughshares, 32 Poems, West Branch, The Greensboro Review,* and on the website *Verse Daily.* She received an M.F.A. from the University of North Carolina at Greensboro and teaches at Queens University of Charlotte.

LISA GLUSKIN's poems have appeared in *The Iowa Review, 32 Poems, ZYZZYVA, Mississippi Review, Bellingham Review,* and *The Cortland Review.* She is the recipient of a Jacob K. Javits Fellowship and a James Duval Phelan Award from the San Francisco Foundation. She lives in San Francisco.

KEVIN A. GONZÁLEZ was born in San Juan, Puerto Rico. His poems have appeared in *Poetry, McSweeney's, Callaloo, The Progressive,* and *North American Review*; and his stories have appeared in *Playboy, Crab Orchard Review,* and *The Virginia Quarterly Review.* Currently, he is a graduate fellow at the Iowa Writers' Workshop.

DANIEL GROVES was born and raised in Narragansett, Rhode Island, and educated at The Johns Hopkins University (B.A., M.A.) and The Ohio State University (M.F.A.). His poems have appeared in *Poetry, The Paris Review, The Yale Review, The Sewanee Theological Review,* and *Smartish Pace.*

JOHN HENNESSY's poetry has appeared or is forthcoming in *The Yale Review, Fulcrum Annual, Ontario Review, Harvard Review, Jacket* (Australia), *LIT,* and *Salt* (UK). He grew up in industrial-strength north Jersey and went to Princeton on a Cane scholarship. For the last few years he has taught undergraduate creative writing and literature courses at the University of Massachusetts, Amherst.

MATTHEW HITTINGER was born in Bethlehem, Pennsylvania, not far from the grave of H.D., and educated at Muhlenberg College and the University of Michigan, where he won a Hopwood Award for Poetry and The Helen S. and John Wagner Prize. His work has appeared or is forthcoming in *American Letters & Commentary, Mantis, Memorious,* and *Fine Madness,* whose editors awarded him their 2004 Kay Deeter Award and nominated him for a Pushcart.

CYNTHIA MARIE HOFFMAN was the 2004–5 Diane Middlebrook Poetry Fellow at the University of Wisconsin-Madison. She received her M.F.A. in poetry from George Mason University, and has been awarded such prizes as the Greg Grummer, Virginia Downs, and Mary Roberts Rinehart. Her work has appeared in *Open City, Margie,* and *Nimrod.*

CARRIE JERRELL received her M.A. from the Writing Seminars at Johns Hopkins University. Her work has appeared or is forthcoming in *32 Poems, The Connecticut Review, The Nebraska Review,* and elsewhere. She is the recipient of two AWP Intro Awards and a Pushcart Prize nomination.

PETER KLINE is a Henry Hoyns Fellow in his third year in the University of Virginia's M.F.A. poetry writing program. He was a finalist for the 2004 Ruth Lilly Fellowship given by *Poetry.* He received his B.A. in English/Poetry Writing from Northwestern

University, where he won the Academy of American Poets Prize in 2000. His poems are forthcoming in *Smartish Pace*.

ANDREW KOZMA currently attends the University of Houston for a Ph.D. in Literature and Creative Writing and is the nonfiction editor for *Gulf Coast*. Poems have appeared or are forthcoming in *Lilies and Cannonballs, Washington Square, Cranky, Spoon River Poetry Review*, and *Rhino*, and his poem "Promises" was nominated for a Pushcart in 2004.

HAILEY LEITHAUSER's work has appeared or is forthcoming in *The Cream City Review, The Gettysburg Review, Meridian, Poetry, Sou'wester*, and other publications, and on *Poetry Daily* and *Verse Daily*. In 2004 she was a winner of the Discovery/*The Nation* Prize and The Elizabeth Matchett Stover Memorial Award from *The Southwest Review*. She is assistant editor of *The National Poetry Review*.

CHIP LIVINGSTON's poetry has appeared recently in *Ploughshares, New American Writing, The New York Quarterly, Barrow Street, Cimarron Review*, and *Stories from the Blue Moon Cafe*. He lives in New York City.

DAVE LUCAS attended John Carroll University and the University of Virginia, where he was a Henry Hoyns Fellow. He received a 2005 Discovery/*The Nation* Prize; other poems have appeared in *Field, Poetry, Slate*, and *The Threepenny Review*. He lives in Cleveland.

DIANE KIRSTEN MARTIN's work has appeared in *Crazyhorse, New England Review, ZYZZYVA, Hayden's Ferry Review, Bellingham Review, Third Coast, North American Review, 32 Poems, Tar River Review, Nimrod, Cutbank*, and other publications. In 2004, her manuscript was chosen by B.H. Fairchild for second place in the *Nimrod*/Hardman Pablo Neruda Prize competition. She lives in San Francisco and was most recently employed as a technical writer.

CLAY MATTHEWS's work has appeared or is forthcoming in *DIAGRAM, Poet Lore, Spork, Diner, New Hampshire Review, storySouth,* and elsewhere. He is currently pursuing a Ph.D. at Oklahoma State while serving as associate editor for the *Cimarron Review.*

A 2004 M.F.A. graduate of the University of Arizona, DAMON MCLAUGHLIN publishes in various online and print journals including *42opus, Stickman Review, North American Review, Indiana Review,* and others. His poem "The Battle of Johnny Freedom" was selected for the anthology of American poets *Red, White, and Blues;* he won this year's *Briar Cliff Review* Annual Poetry Contest for his poem "Ceremony."

MICHAEL MEINHARDT is a graduate student of the University of Wisconsin-Milwaukee program. He relinquished promising careers as refuse collector, lingerie model, and strip club bouncer to follow his heart.

SALLY MOLINI's work has appeared or is forthcoming in *Tar River Poetry, North Carolina Literary Review, Karamu, Margie,* and elsewhere. She earned an M.F.A. from Warren Wilson College and lives in Omaha, Nebraska.

STEVE MUESKE holds an M.F.A. in Writing from Hamline University and has published poems recently in *Water-Stone, The American Poetry Journal, 88, Northeast Review,* and elsewhere. His first chapbook is *Whatever the Story Requires.*

CARRIE OEDING is a doctoral student in creative writing/poetry at The Ohio University. She received an M.F.A. in poetry from the Inland Northwest Center for Writers at Eastern Washington University in Spokane, Washington. Her work has appeared in such places as *Third Coast, South Dakota Review,* and is forthcoming in *The Greensboro Review* in fall 2005. Oeding is also the recipient of The Ohio University's Emerson Poetry Prize.

"Countryfied" is THOMAS PARK's first published poem. He currently attends Wayne State University.

CECILY PARKS is a graduate of the M.F.A. program at Columbia University. Her poems have appeared or are forthcoming in *Five Points, New England Review, Southwest Review, The Virginia Quarterly Review, Yale Review,* and elsewhere. Her chapbook *Cold Work* was selected by Li-Young Lee for the 2005 Poetry Society of America New York Chapbook Fellowship and will be published in December 2005.

JOANNA PEARSON graduated from the University of North Carolina at Chapel Hill in 2002, where she won the Robert B. House Memorial Prize in Poetry and was a finalist for the Ruth Lilly Fellowship sponsored by *Poetry.* She earned her M.A. in Anglo-Irish literature from University College Dublin. Currently a student at the Johns Hopkins University School of Medicine, she recently won the William Carlos Williams poetry contest for medical students in the United States and Canada.

SHANN RAY teaches at Gonzaga University. "A Quiet Poem about Marital Sex" is his first published poem. His essays and fiction have appeared in *Narrative Magazine, Talking River Review, The Greenleaf Voices Series, StoryQuarterly,* and *McSweeney's.* His wife wears the garment of praise instead of the spirit of despair. His daughters shine like the sun.

LAUREN RUSK's publications include poems in *The Café Review, Saint Elizabeth Street, Sequoia,* and the *Cloud View Poets* anthology in the United States, and in *Fire* and *The Interpreter's House* in England, as well as a book of criticism, *The Life Writing of Otherness: Woolf, Baldwin, Kingston, and Winterson.* She teaches modern and contemporary literature in Stanford University's Continuing Studies Program and lives part of each year in Oxford, England.

LESLIE SHIPMAN's work has appeared in the *Red Rock Review, Cortland Review,* and *The Laurel Review;* and is forthcoming in *Bellingham Review.* She is currently enrolled in the M.F.A. Program for Writers at Warren Wilson College. She lives with her daughter in Chappaqua, New York.

ELEANOR STANFORD's poems have appeared in *Poetry, Ploughshares, Indiana Review,* and other journals. She received her M.F.A. from the University of Virginia and lives in Philadelphia.

LAURIE STOLL's work is forthcoming in *Streetlight.* She lives in Charlottesville, Virginia.

LAURA-GRAY STREET's work has appeared in *Blackbird, ISLE, Shenandoah, Meridian, The Notre Dame Review, The Greensboro Review, Poetry Daily, From the Fishouse,* and elsewhere, and has been commissioned by the New York Festival of Song. Educated at Hollins University, the University of Virginia, and the Warren Wilson M.F.A. Program for Writers, she is now an assistant professor of English at Randolph-Macon Woman's College in Lynchburg, Virginia.

IRA SUKRUNGRUANG is a first generation Thai-American born and raised in Chicago. His work has appeared in *Witness, North American Review, Another Chicago Magazine,* and numerous other literary journals. He is the coeditor of *What Are You Looking At? The First Fat Fiction Anthology* (Harvest Books, 2003) and *Scoot Over, Skinny: The Fat Nonfiction Anthology* (Harvest Books, 2005). He teaches creative writing at State University of New York Oswego.

DUFFIE TAYLOR attends Hollins University, where she has studied with R.H.W. Dillard and Dara Wier.

CODY WALKER teaches English at the University of Washington and poetry as part of Seattle Arts and Lectures' Writers in the Schools program. His work has appeared or is forthcoming in *Shenandoah, Prairie Schooner, Hayden's Ferry Review, Margie, The Cream City Review, The Madison Review,* and elsewhere.

ELLEN WEHLE has poems upcoming in *Gulf Coast, Poetry International, The Iowa Review, The Southern Review,* and *The New Republic.* She lives in Winthrop, Massachusetts, where she walks the beach every morning with her spaniel, Mickey.

Acknowledgements

Dan Albergotti's "Stones And Shadows" previously appeared in *The Greensboro Review*

Beth Bachmann's "Another Poem about Memphis Rocking" previously appeared in
The Southern Review

Tama Baldwin's "Bad Weather" previously appeared in *Poetry International*

Sandra Beasley's "After Miscarriage" previously appeared in *Reed*

Paula Bohince's "The Fly" previously appeared in *AGNI*

Allen Braden's "First Elk, 1939" previously appeared in *The Virginia Quarterly Review*

Jennifer Chang's "Conversation with Owl and Clouds" previously appeared in
New England Review

Jennifer Chapis's "After Ovarian Surgery" previously appeared in *The GSU Review*

Carol Ann Davis's "Distal" previously appeared in *The Southern Review*

Julie Funderburk's "Without Power" previously appeared in *The Greensboro Review*

Kevin A. González's "Cultural Slut" previously appeared in *Hotel Amerika*

Daniel Groves's "A Stranger Here Myself" previously appeared in *Smartish Pace*

John Hennessy's "Why Not Dig Up the Dog?" previously appeared in *Fulcrum 3*

Matthew Hittinger's "The Fresco Worker Appears Suddenly in the Picture"
previously appeared in *Memorius.*

Cynthia Marie Hoffman's "Dear Alexander Nevsky," previously appeared in *Phoebe*

Carrie Jerrell's "When the Rider Is Truth" previously appeared in *32 Poems*

Hailey Leithauser's "The Moon Speaks of Alzheimer's" previously appeared in
The Antioch Review

Chip Livingston's "Burn" previously appeared in *Ploughshares*

Dave Lucas's "Epithalamium" previously appeared in *The Threepenny Review*

Diane Kirsten Martin's "Mom Poem" previously appeared in *Nimrod*

Clay Matthews's "Scissors" previously appeared in *Softblow*

Damon McLaughlin's "Ceremony" previously appeared in *The Briar Cliff Review*

Sally Molini's "Silk Shop on the Ganges" previously appeared in *Tar River Poetry*

Steve Mueske's "On Poetics" previously appeared in *The Massachusetts Review*

Carrie Oeding's "The Women Wear Black" previously appeared in *Third Coast*

Cecily Parks's "Self-Portrait as Angler's Dragonfly" previously appeared in
    The Virginia Quarterly Review
Laurie Stoll's "In the Details" previously appeared in *Streetlight*
Laura-Gray Street's "Ring-Necks" previously appeared in *Blackbird*
Ira Sukrungruang's "In Thailand It Is Night" previously appeared in *Ninth Letter*
Cody Walker's "Bozo Sapphics" previously appeared in *Pontoon*
Ellen Wehle's "Reincarnation" previously appeared in *The Grove Review*

Participating Writing Programs

American University
M.F.A. Program in Creative Writing
Department of Literature
4400 Massachusetts Avenue N.W.
Washington, DC 20036

Bowling Green State University
Creative Writing Program
Department of English
Bowling Green, OH 43403
www.bgsu.edu/departments/
    creative-writing/home.html

Brown University
Program in Literary Arts
Box 1923
Providence, RI 02912
www.brown.edu/Departments/
    Literary_Arts

Columbia University Writing Division
School of the Arts
Dodge Hall
2960 Broadway, Room 400
New York, NY 10027-6902

Creative Writing Program
University of Tennessee at Chattanooga
English Department
615 McCallie Avenue
Chattanooga, TN 37411

Emerson College
M.F.A. in Creative Writing
120 Boylston Street
Boston, MA 02116-1596

Fine Arts Work Center in Provincetown
24 Pearl Street
Provincetown, MA 02657
www.fawc.org

Florida International University
M.F.A. Program in Creative Writing
Department of English
Biscayne Bay Camp
3000 N.E. 151st Street
North Miami, FL 33181

George Mason University
Graduate Creative Writing Program
4400 University Drive
MSN 3E4
Fairfax, VA 22030
creativewriting.gmu.edu

Louisiana State University
English Department, 213 Allen
Baton Rouge, LA 70803

McNeese State University
Program in Creative Writing
P.O. Box 92655
Lake Charles, LA 70609
www.mfa.mcneese.edu

Minnesota State University, Mankato
Creative Writing Program
230 Armstrong Hall
Mankato, MN 56001
www.english.mnsu.edu

Sarah Lawrence College
Office of Graduate Studies
1 Mead Way
Bronxville, NY 10708-5999

Sewanee Writers' Conference
735 University Avenue
Sewanee, TN 37383-1000
www.sewaneewriters.org

Stanford University
Creative Writing Program
Department of English
Bldg 460 Rm 218
Stanford, CA 94305-2087
www.stanford.edu/dept/english/cw

The Asian American Writers' Workshop
16 West 32nd Street Suite 10A
New York, NY 10001
www.aaww.org

The Bread Loaf Writers' Conference
Middlebury College
Kirk Alumni Center
Middlebury, VT 05753
www.middlebury.edu

The Loft Literary Center
Mentor Series Program
Suite 200, Open Book
1011 Washington Avenue
South Minneapolis, MN 55414-1246
www.loft.org

The New School
Graduate Writing Program
66 West 12th Street, Room 508
New York, NY 10001

University of Alaska
Fairbanks Program in Creative Writing
Department of English
P.O. Box 755720
Fairbanks, AK 99775-5720
www.uaf.edu/english

University of Arizona
Creative Writing Program
Department of English
Modern Languages Bldg. #67
Tucson, AZ 85721-0067

University of Arkansas
Program in Creative Writing
Department of English
333 Kimpel Hall
Fayetteville, AR 72701
www.uark.edu/depts/english/PCWT.html

University of Georgia
Creative Writing Program
English Department
Park Hall 111
Athens, GA 30602-6205

University of Hawaii
Creative Writing Program
English Department
1733 Donaghho Road
Honolulu, HI 96822
www.english.hawaii.edu/cw

University of Idaho
Creative Writing Program
Department of English
Moscow, ID 83843-1102
www.class.uidaho.edu/english/
    CW/mfaprogram.html

University of Illinois at Chicago
Program for Writers
Department of English MC/162
601 South Morgan Street
Chicago, IL 60607-7120
www.uic.edu/english

University of Iowa
Program in Creative Writing
102 Dey House
507 North Clinton Street
Iowa City, IA 52242

University of Louisiana at Lafayette
Creative Writing Concentration
Department of English, P.O. Box 44691
Lafayette, LA 70504-4691
www.louisiana.edu/Academic/
    LiberalArts/ENGL/Creative.html

University of Maryland
Creative Writing Program
Department of English
3119F Susquehanna Hall
College Park, MD 20742
www.english.umd.edu/
    programs/CreateWriting

University of Missouri-Columbia
Program in Creative Writing
Department of English
107 Tate Hall
Columbia, MO 65211

University of Missouri-St. Louis
Master of Fine Arts in Creative Writing Program
Department of English
8001 Natural Bridge Road
St. Louis, MO 63121

University of Nebraska, Lincoln
Creative Writing Program
Department of English
202 Andrews Hall
Lincoln, NE 68588-0333

University of North Carolina, Greensboro
M.F.A. Writing Program
Dept. of English, 134 McIver Building
P.O. Box 26170
Greensboro, NC 27402-6170
www.uncg.edu/eng/mfa

University of Notre Dame
Creative Writing Program
356 O'Shaughnessy Hall
Notre Dame, IN 46556-0368
www.nd.edu/~alcwp

University of Oregon
Program in Creative Writing
Box 5243
Eugene, OR 97403-5243
darkwing.uoregon.edu/~crwrweb

University of Virginia
Creative Writing Program
Department of English
P.O. Box 400121
Charlottesville, VA 22904-4121
www.engl.virginia.edu/cwp

University of Washington
Creative Writing Program
Box 354330
Seattle, WA 98195-4330

University of West Florida
Department of English
11000 University Parkway
Pensacola, FL 32514

University of Wyoming
Creative Writing Program
Department of English
P.O. Box 3353
Laramie, WY 82071-2000
www.uwyo.edu/creativewriting

Wayne State University
Creative Writing Program
English Department
Detroit, MI 48202

West Virginia University
Creative Writing Program
Department of English
P.O. Box 6269
Morgantown, WV 26506-6269
www.as.wvu.edu/english

Wichita State University
M.F.A. in Creative Writing
1845 North Fairmount
Wichita, KS 67260-0014
webs.wichita.edu/cwfwww

Canada

The Humber School for Writers
205 Humber College Boulevard
Humber College
Toronto, ON M9W 5L7
www.humber.ca/creativeandperformingarts

University of Victoria
Bachelor of Fine Arts
Department of Writing
P.O. Box 1700, STN CSC
Victoria, BC V8W 2Y2

University of British Columbia
Creative Writing Program
Buchanan E462-1866 Main Mall
Vancouver, BC V6T 1Z1
www.creativewriting.ubc.ca

Participating Magazines

African American Review
Saint Louis University
Humanities 317
3800 Lindell Boulevard
St. Louis, MO 63108-3414
aar.slu.edu

Alligator Juniper
220 Grove Avenue
Prescott, AZ 86301

American Poetry Review
117 South 17th Street
Suite 910
Philadelphia, PA 19103

Another Chicago Magazine
3709 N. Kenmore
Chicago, IL 60630
www.anotherchicagomagazine.com

Antioch Review
P.O. Box 148
Yellow Springs, OH 45387

Arts & Letters
Georgia College & State University
Campus Box 89
Milledgeville, GA 31061
al.gcsu.edu

Bellingham Review
Western Washington University
MS-9053
Bellingham, WA 98225
www.wwu.edu/~bhreview

Beloit Poetry Journal
The Beloit Poetry Journal Foundation, Inc.
P.O. Box 151
Farmington, ME 04938
www.bpj.org

Black Warrior Review
University of Alabama
Black Warrior Review
Box 862936
Tuscaloosa, AL 35486
www.webdelsol.com/bwr

Blackbird
Virginia Commonwealth University
Department of English
P.O. Box 843082
Richmond, VA 23284-3082
www.blackbird.vcu.edu

Calyx,
A Journal of Art and Literature by Women
CALYX, Inc.
P.O. Box B
Corvallis, OR 97339
www.proaxis.com/~calyx

Field
Oberlin College Press
50 North Professor Street
Oberlin, OH 44074

Gulf Stream Magazine
English Department
FIU Biscayne Bay Campus
3000 NE 151 Street
North Miami, FL 33181-3000

Harvard Review
Harvard University
Lamont Library
Cambridge, MA 02138
hcl.harvard.edu/houghton/
    departments/harvardreview

Hotel Amerika
Ohio University
English Dept. / 360 Ellis Hall
Athens, OH 45701
www.hotelamerika.net

Hunger Mountain
Vermont College
36 College Street
Montpelier, VT 05602

Indiana Review
Indiana University
Ballantine Hall 465
1020 E. Kirkwood Ave.
Bloomington, IN 47405-7103
www.indiana.edu/~inreview

Memorius
1 Fitchburg St. #C518
Somerville, MA 02143
www.memorious.org

Michigan Quarterly Review
University of Michigan
3574 Rackham Bldg.
915 East Washington St.
Ann Arbor, MI 48019-1070

Mid-American Review
Bowling Green State University
Department of English
Box W
Bowling Green, OH 43403

New Letters
University of Missouri-Kansas City
5101 Rockhill Road
Kansas City, MO 64110
www.newletters.org

New Orleans Review
Loyola University
Box 195
New Orleans, LA 70118
www.loyno.edu/~noreview

Nimrod
The University of Tulsa
600 South College
Tulsa, OK 74104-3189
www.utulsa.edu/nimrod

Ninth Letter
234 English, Univ. of Illinois
608 S. Wright St.
Urbana, IL 61801
www.ninthletter.com

Northwest Review
University of Oregon
369 PLC New Line
Eugene, OR 97403

Pheobe
George Mason University
4400 University Drive
Fairfax, VA 22030-4444

Pleiades
Central Missouri State University
Department of English and Philosophy
Warrensburg, MO 64093
www.cmsu.edu/englphil/pleiades

Ploughshares
Emerson College
120 Boylston St.
Boston, MA 02116
www.pshares.org

Poetry International
San Diego State University
Department of English
  & Comparative Literature
5500 Campanile
San Diego, CA 92182-8140

River Styx
634 North Grand Boulevard
Twelfth Floor
Saint Louis, MO 63103

Seneca Review
Hobart and William Smith Colleges
Geneva, NY 14456
www.hws.edu/SenecaReview

Shenandoah
Washington and Lee University
Troubadour Theater
2nd Floor, Box W
Lexington, VA 24450-0303
shenandoah.wlu.edu

The Greensboro Review
University of North Carolina, Greensboro
English Department
134 McIver, P.O. Box 26170
Greensboro, NC 27402-6170
www.greensbororeview.com

The Hudson Review
684 Park Avenue
New York, NY 10021
www.hudsonreview.com

The Kenyon Review
Kenyon College
Walton House
Gambier, OH 43022-9623
www.kenyonreview.org

The Powhatan Review
4936 Farrington Drive
Virginia Beach, VA 23455
powhatanreview.com

The Southern Review
Louisiana State University
43 Allen Hall
Baton Rouge, LA 70803
www.lsu.edu/thesouthernreview

The Southwest Review
Southern Methodist University
307 Fondren Library West
P.O. Box 750374
Dallas, TX 75275-0374
www.southwestreview.org

The Virginia Quarterly Review
University of Virginia
One West Range
P.O. Box 400223
Charlottesville, VA 22904
www.vqronline.org

The William & Mary Review
William & Mary
P.O. Box 8795
Williamsburg, VA 23187-8795

Third Coast
Western Michigan University
Department of English
Kalamazoo, MI 49008-5092

Washington Square
New York University
Creative Writing Program
19 University Place
Room 219, NY 10003-4556

ZYZZYVA
P.O. Box 590069
San Francisco, CA 94159-0069
www.zyzzyva.org

Canada

Descant
P.O. Box 314
Station P
Toronto, ON M5S 2S8
www.descant.on.ca